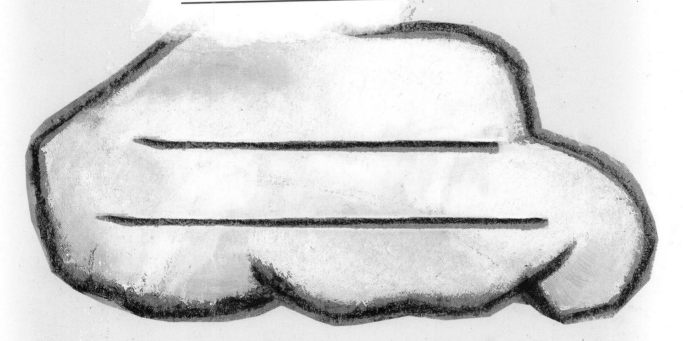

For my little Else.
A kiss from your giant - C.N.

Text copyright © 2004 Carl Norac
Illustrations copyright © 2004 Ingrid Godon
Moral rights asserted
Dual language copyright © 2004 Mantra Lingua
All rights reserved
A CIP record for this book is available
from the British Library.

First published in 2004 by Macmillan Children's Books, London
First dual language publication in 2004 by Mantra Lingua

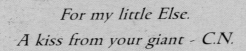

mantra

5 Alexandra Grove, London N12 8NU
www.mantralingua.com

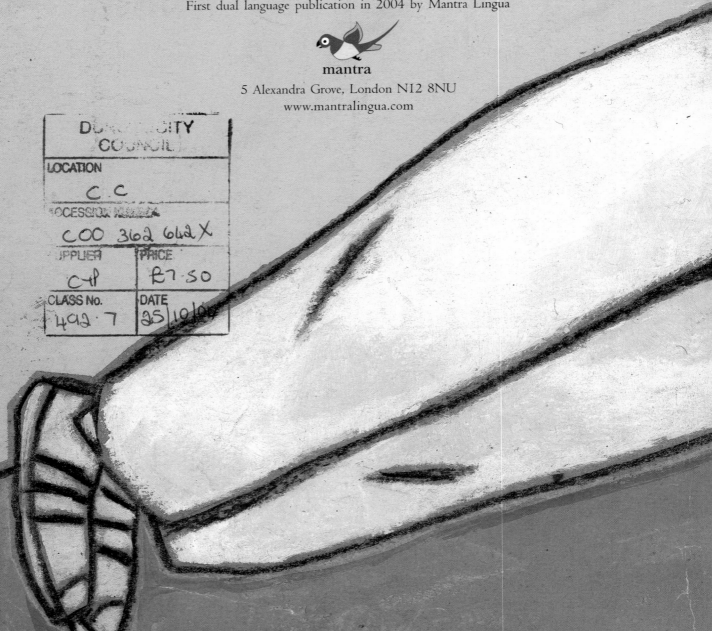

CARL NORAC

INGRID GODON

أبى العملاق

My Daddy is a Giant

Arabic translation by Samy Daoud

mantra

إن أبى عملاق.
عندما أريد حضنه،
أضطر أن أستعمل سلّماً.

My daddy is a giant.
When I want to cuddle him,
I have to climb a ladder.

عندما نلعب لعبة الأستغماية،
يجب على أبى أن يختبئ
خلف جبلٍ.

When we play hide-and-seek,
my daddy has to hide
behind a mountain.

تنام السحب
على أكتاف أبى
عندما تتعب .

And when the clouds are tired,
they come and sleep
on my daddy's shoulders.

عندما يعطس أبى،
إنه كالإعصار
الذى يهبّ بالبحر بعيداً.

When my daddy sneezes,
it's like a hurricane.
It blows the sea away.

عندما يضحك أبى،
إنه كإعصار أخر
الذى يطيِّر أوراق الأشجار كلها.

When my daddy laughs,
it's like another hurricane.
All the leaves fly off the trees.

تحب الطيور أبى،
وتبنى أعشاشها
فى شعره.

Birds love my daddy.
They make their nests
in his hair.

أبى دائماً يفوز
عندما نلعب كرة القدم.
بإستطاعته رفس الكرة
عالياً كعلو القمر.

When we play football,
my daddy always wins.

He can kick the ball as high as the moon.

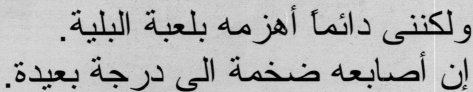

ولكنني دائماً أهزمه بلعبة البلية.
إن أصابعه ضخمة الى درجة بعيدة.

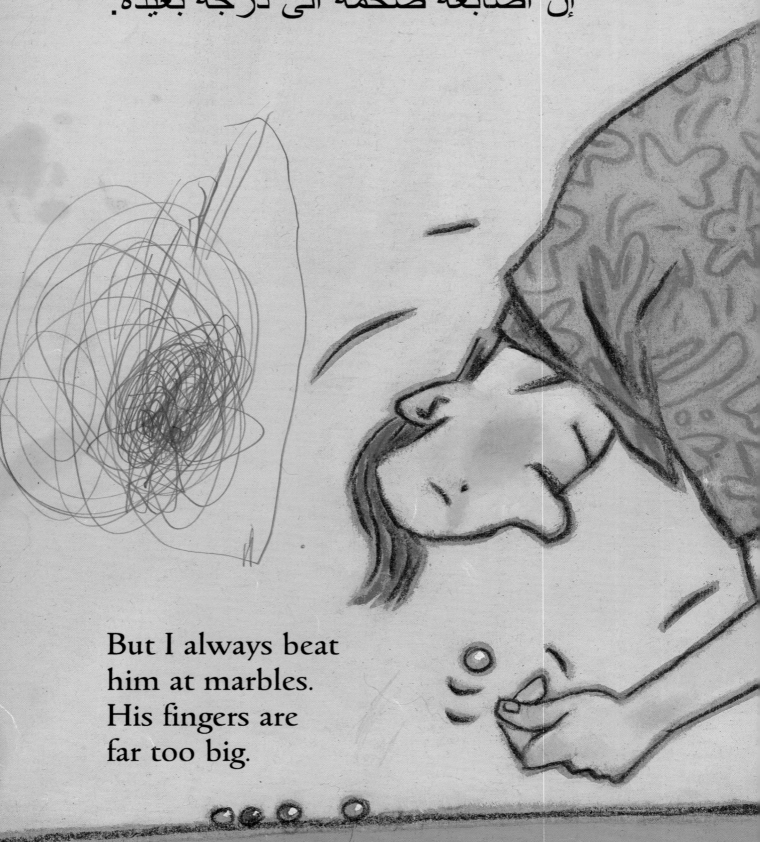

But I always beat
him at marbles.
His fingers are
far too big.

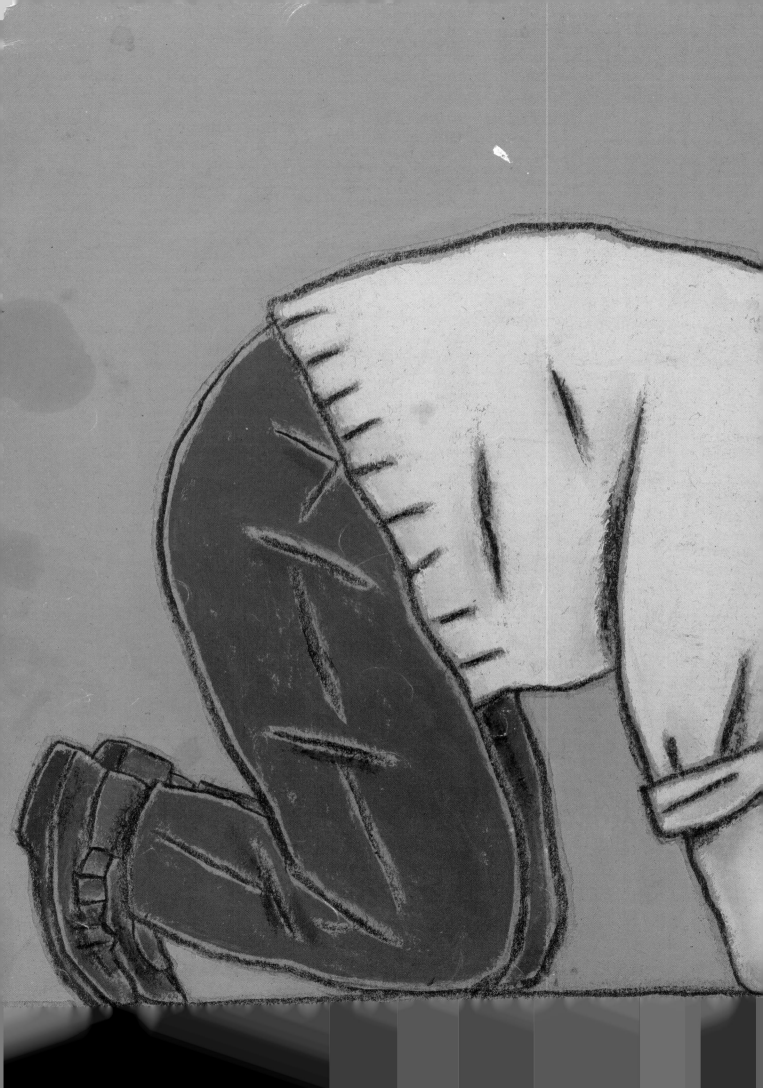

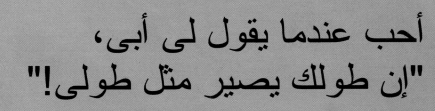

أحب عندما يقول لى أبى،
"إن طولك يصير مثل طولى!"

I like it when my
daddy says,
"You're getting as
tall as me!"

عندما يركض أبى،
تهتز الأرض
كأنها خائفة.

When my daddy runs,

the ground shakes

as if it was scared.

ولكننى لا أخاف
من أى شئ
عندما أكون بحضن أبى.

But I'm not scared
of anything when
I'm in my daddy's arms.

إن أبى عملاق،
ويحبّنى من كل
قلبه الضخم.

My daddy is a giant,
and he loves me with
all his giant heart.

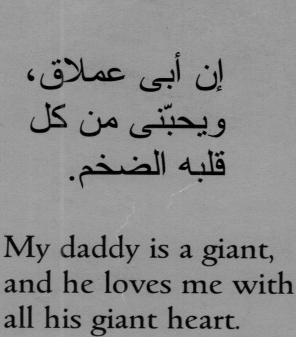